Caroline Righton's

CREATE IT

WITH

WAX, CLAY & PLASTER

IN AN

EVENING

NEXUS SPECIAL INTERESTS

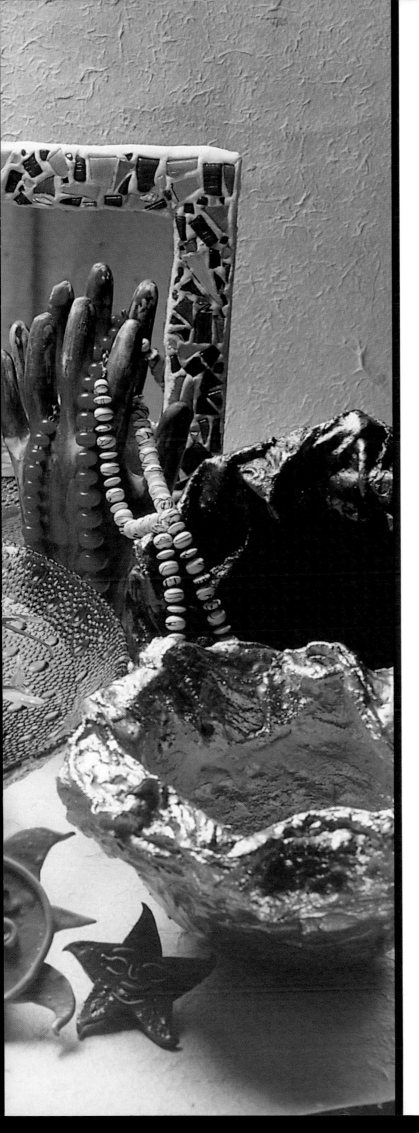

Caroline Righton's

CREATE IT
WITH
WAX, CLAY & PLASTER
IN AN
EVENING

DESIGNER
ELAINE DONOVAN
PHOTOGRAPHER
RICHARD LAING

NEXUS SPECIAL INTERESTS

Nexus Special Interests Ltd.
Nexus House
Azalea Drive
Swanley
Kent BR8 8HU
England

First published in Great Britain by Nexus Special Interests Ltd., 1998

ISDN 1-85486-177-8

Dedicated to our mother

Colour separations by PDQ, Bungay, Suffolk
Printed and bound in Great Britain by Jarrold Book Printing, Thetford, Norfolk

CONTENTS

Introduction   **7**
About this book   **8**

Wax
Introduction   **11**

Origins   12
Equipment   14
Inspiration   16
Techniques   18
Step-by-Step   20
Projects   22
Other Ideas   28

Clay
Introduction   **31**

Origins   32
Equipment   34
Inspiration   36
Techniques   38
Step-by-Step   40
Projects   42
Other Ideas   48

Plaster
Introduction   **51**

Origins   52
Equipment   54
Inspiration   56
Techniques   58
Step-by-Step   60
Projects   62
Other Ideas   68

Kits   **70**
Index   **71**
Equipment and Suppliers   **72**

INTRODUCTION

Life today can be so hectic that spare time is all the more precious, and while it would be easy to spend that spare time catching up on the domestic chores or doing extra shopping, I bet you wish you could just take a bit of time out for you occasionally and lose yourself in something absorbing and creative.

The trouble is - by the time you've got yourself organised to do anything productive it's time to stop again and you have to leave it half finished because of all the other demands on your time.

Well this book is for you - all the craft ideas in it are 'do-able' in a few hours. Believe me I've done them! If you add a call to your local craft store or artists' suppliers shop to your supermarket dash, then by the end of the day you should have created something for yourself, your home or as a gift. More importantly you will have spent a lovely creative evening which has relaxed you and certainly taken your mind off the million and one other things your children, your partner, your boss etc. want you to worry about

Creating something in an evening using modelling materials such as clay, wax or plaster is easy and really enjoyable. Modern materials mean you don't need expensive equipment and even if your item doesn't turn out quite as you planned, the act of shaping and moulding will be very therapeutic.

My favourite for de-stressing has got to be working with clay. All the projects in this book use the self-hardening material so you have no need of a kiln. Making things with plaster has a magic all its own. I love the way the sloshy liquid transforms so quickly into a pure white hard shape. If, like me, you don't wait for special days and holidays to light candles in your home, then you will never buy them again once you have found out how easy it is to make your own from wax. Have fun!

7

WAX, CLAY
AND
PLASTER

There are nine different projects in this book using wax, clay and plaster – all of them easily achievable in an evening.

WAX

For such an easy and effective craft, wax candlemaking wrongly seems to have got a reputation for being difficult. I can promise you that you'll be thrilled at how quickly you can make your own candles - not just plain boring ones either. While the basic candlemaking technique is common to all three project suggestions, I offer some ideas that you can adapt to truly individualise the candles you make. Take your inspiration from nature and look for natural containers such as shells to fill with wax or leaves to wrap around the outside of the candle. Or, during the melting and making stage, add herbs and scents so that a restful or energising aroma accompanies your candlelight.

CLAY

If, like me, you have always felt a bit daunted by the idea of making items with clay, then don't be. You really don't need to fire your finished items in a kiln. Look in your local craft shop for the various self-hardening clays or the modelling materials you can bake in your oven at home. My projects in this book include a very easy flat worked picture frame which you can personalise with your own words, some fun fridge magnets which have proved invaluable for leaving messages for the various family members, and a sweet trinket pot.

PLASTER OF PARIS

I first used Plaster of Paris during my Art A-level course and actually made a ring hand just like the one I've included as one of the projects. It lasted for years and was really useful and I don't know why it has taken me so long to get around to making another one. The secret with plaster moulds is always to make sure they are flexible - the shapes around the picture frame are actually from ice-cube trays. Plaster is a versatile medium, and to prove the point the bowls are made from kitchen cloths soaked in plaster!

9

WAX

I hope the three wax candle projects I've suggested will inspire you to come up with your own themes and ideas. The simplest project is probably the floating candles ... and the cheapest too. But the candles with leaves, spices and fruit decorations do make stunning gifts and are very easy to make, while the shell candles work beautifully at individual place settings on your dinner table and will impress your guests even though they will only take you seconds to make.

11

T H E   O R I G I N S   O F   W A X

The dictionary definition of wax says it all - wax is a pliable substance of animal, plant, mineral or synthetic origin! It melts at high temperatures of between 35 and 100 degrees Celsius and then forms a hard film. It therefore comes as no surprise to discover that because it has so many sources it has also had a multitude of uses as far back in history as man himself.

The most obvious use of wax, and certainly the interest we have in this book, is as candles and we know from unearthed Egyptian candlesticks that candles were being used for light as far back as 3,000 BC. The wax for them probably came from bees. Today, beeswax is the most widely distributed and important animal wax. It forms the cell walls of the honeycomb and a bee has to consume between 6-10 pounds of honey for each pound of wax. Beeswax candles are most likely to be found in churches - indeed some ordinances insist upon it. Wax from the sperm whale is also widely recorded for its use for candlemaking.

Primitive civilisations elsewhere in the world might have discovered the properties of wax as found in the plant world. The *Balanophora* and *Langsdorffia* flower stems, native to South America, contain a flammable waxy substance that even today is used as candles by some communities. Only a few vegetable waxes are produced in commercial quantities such as Carnauba wax, which comes from the surface of the fronds of a type of Brazilian palm tree.

In the mountainous regions of Utah, Poland and Romania wax is retrieved from rocks. This is called ozokerite and runs as veins, filling fissures in the rock.

However, the most universally used wax today is paraffin wax. This accounts for 90 per cent of the wax used in the world and is often blended with other chemicals depending on its use. It comes from petroleum and was first produced commercially in 1867, less than 10 years after the first petroleum well was drilled. Synthetic paraffin wax was introduced after the Second World War. Candles are most likely to be made using a combination of paraffin and stearic acid.

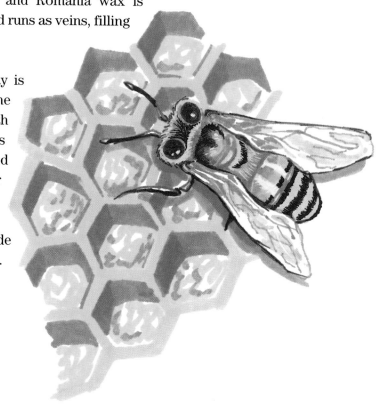

Although wax is used for a million different things from cosmetics to flooring, we are most familiar with it when used in candlemaking and its ability to provide mankind with light has, historically speaking, probably been its most important function.

As well as being used domestically it has also had other functions. As the Phoenicians navigated the seas trading their fine wares so the first lighthouses were being built, and it is known that candles were used in massive lanterns with panes of glass or horn from the first century AD. However, there were disadvantages - the smoke from the candles tended to blacken the glass or thin horn that was used in the lanterns.

In fact, the 'International Candle' has been used as a measurement of light source and in geographical terms it was calculated that the light of 10,000 candles would be visible at 18 miles in clear weather. The measurement was originally defined as a one-sixth pound candle made from sperm whale wax burning at the rate of 120 grains per hour.

With the fantastic light shows of today's concerts and theatres it's hard to imagine what it must have been like when actors and other performers relied on the light of front-of-stage candles for the audience to appreciate their performances. Not that it restricted their efforts to create special effects - in 1545, an Italian theatrical impresario told his stage manager to place the candles behind glass flasks filled with amber and blue coloured water.

You can sculpt and mould wax if you keep the items quite small. The Victorians used to keep carved or moulded pieces of wax fruit under glass domes. Today, you can see fruit and other shapes moulded from wax but more often than not there will be a wick sticking out of the top. It seems we like our wax mainly in candle form these days!

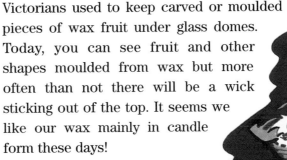

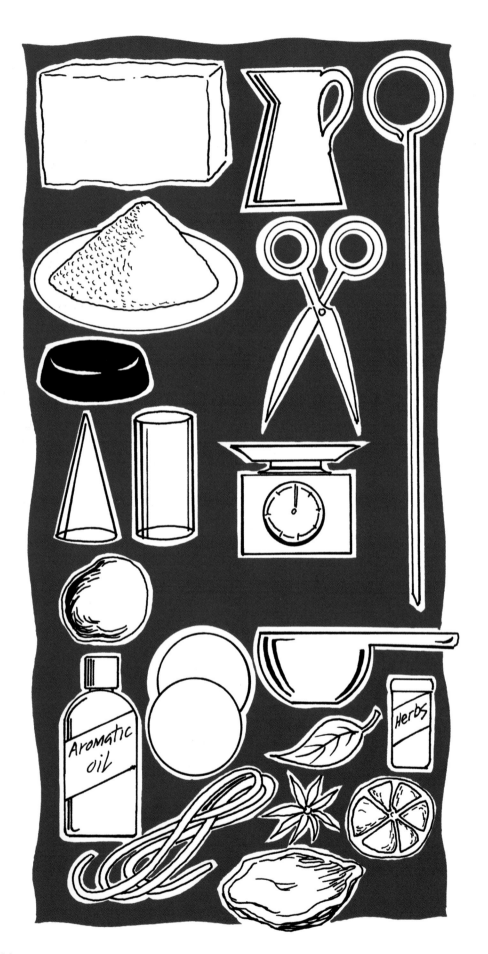

Paraffin wax

Stearin

Candle dye

Moulds

Mould seal

Aromatic oil or essence

Wicks

Wick discs

Rods

Jug

Scissors

Scales

Pans

Herbs, leaves, flowers, dried
orange etc.

Shells

EQUIPMENT

The equipment you need to make things from wax is quite straightforward and readily available from craft shops.

Paraffin wax in block or granular form is the cheapest and most readily available. You can always add a small amount of beeswax that can be bought in block form, gives off a nice smell and helps it burn evenly.

Heat source on top of your cooker.

Stearin or **stearic acid** is an important wax additive. It dissolves wax dyes, adds colour clarity and helps the wax pop out of its mould. Add stearin to wax in 1:10 proportions.

Candle dye comes in block or powder form and you dissolve it during the heating process.

Moulds can be bought in all sorts of different shapes, but before you buy one look around at home and see what you might already have such as flexible bottle tops, plastic bottles that can be cut etc.

Mould seal or plastic clay to seal the wick hole at the base of the mould.

Aromatic oils and **essences**. I love to scent my candles with a few drops of lavender, vanilla or rosemary candle oil.

Wicks can be bought in various thicknesses by the metre or in pre-cut lengths. My advice is to buy the more rigid pre-waxed and pre-cut wicking until you get the hang of the craft.

Wick discs hold the wick in place at the base and in the centre of the wax. You can cut your own from thin metal or even use a small button or washer.

Rods. Again these can be bought, although a skewer, knitting or crochet needle will do the job just as well to loosely tie the tops of the wick around at the top of your mould to keep it straight.

Pans. A double boiler is the best because wax over a direct flame can very easily overheat and catch fire.

Jug. You don't really need this as long as your pans have a lip for pouring although a small jug gives you more control when pouring the liquid wax.

Scissors for trimming the wick.

Scales for measuring out the quantities of wax and stearin etc.

Shells or indeed any other suitable container to pour your wax into, unless you want it to be freestanding and popped out of its mould.

Herbs. The same reason as for oils and essence.

Leaves, flowers etc. to decorate the outside of your candles.

Now what sort of candle to make? Well, I would let an occasion or a situation dictate the answer. Are you having a party that is crying out for individual candles on the place settings or a stunning centrepiece of floating candles? Is there a corner of your bedroom or bathroom where an aromatic candle could help create a particular mood? Is it near Christmas, Easter or Harvest where a seasonal candle bedecked with nature's emblems might be appropriate? I just love candlelight, and really need no excuses to light them all over the house whether there is an occasion or not!

TECHNIQUES

A word of caution before you start to make any candles - hot wax can give you a nasty burn so keep safety considerations uppermost when you are melting the wax. Keep a damp tea-towel handy so that you can cover the pan if the wax should catch fire. Never leave the pan unattended and keep the outside surfaces free of wax drips. All that said, if you follow the instructions carefully, you should have no problems.

Once you have mastered basic candlemaking as explained in the step-by-step instructions on page 20, you can try out some different methods.

MULTICOLOURED

For example, you can make multicoloured candles by first making an accurate measurement of the volume of your mould with water and then dividing that by the number of colours you want to use. Pour each layer in the normal way, waiting in between layers for the wax to begin to set and a skin to form. Poke some holes in the surface of the layer with a skewer so that the next colour will run into them and be anchored.

WHIPPED WAX

You can get a really different end result by whipping your wax before moulding. Prepare the wax as normal and have the mould ready. Pour the liquid wax into a mixing bowl and when it has cooled a bit and a thick skin has formed whisk it up into a light foam with a whisk or a fork. Pack this quickly into your mould using a flat-bladed knife. As soon as the mould is full push a skewer through the centre so that you can feed a wick through. Seal around the wick hole with a little more melted wax and rough the top up so it is not smooth. When the candle is set and removed from its mould you can apply an extra outer coat of whipped wax, again with a knife or spatula.

B E E S W A X

If you are slightly put off candlemaking by the thought of having to work with hot melted wax you can still make your own candles from beeswax sheeting which does not need to be melted at all. You can buy it from any good candlemaking equipment supplier and you simply fold one edge of the beeswax sheet over a length of wick before rolling it gently and firmly into a sausage shape. Seal the edge to the candle by pressing firmly with your finger and trim the wick allowing about 5mm to stick out at the top.

D E C O R A T I O N

You can decorate the surface of a candle with just about anything. Small Christmas decorations can be stuck on with glue and glitter, and sequins will catch the light prettily, but my favourite is to use leaves, bark, dried citrus fruits, ferns and herbs. The best way to apply these is simple. Glue them lightly into place and then quickly dip the candle into molten white paraffin wax. This will seal the decoration and help it to retain its colour.

STEP-BY-STEP

The kitchen really is the ideal candlemaking workroom. Not only is it the place where you are most likely to have a heat source but a glance around it will reveal all manner of glasses, cartons, bottles, pots and even boxes that can be used as moulds. All you need to buy are the basic materials.

Remember, if it all goes horribly wrong you can always melt down and start again!

THE MOULD

You can buy cheap candle moulds from a craft shop but you can also make your own at home from yogurt pots, waxed paper cartons or even plastic rainwater pipes. If you need to add a base you can improvise one from a tin or jam jar lid, carefully sealing it with clay or special candle mould seal.

THE WICK

If you haven't bought pre-waxed wicks it will help to dip the length of wicking you need into some melted white wax first and let it dry so that you can easily pull it taut when it is secured in the mould. You need to secure the wick at the top and bottom of the mould so that it stands straight when you pour in the melted wax. Tie a knot at one end of the wicking and thread it through the base of the mould. Pull it taut and seal the hole outside with some mould seal. You can use a wick disc. Tie the other end of the wick around a skewer tightly enough so the skewer rests across the top of the mould and the wick is taut. If you can't pierce a hole in the bottom of the mould you can pierce a hole right through after your candle is made and thread a wick through, filling up the hole with liquid wax.

MELTING THE WAX

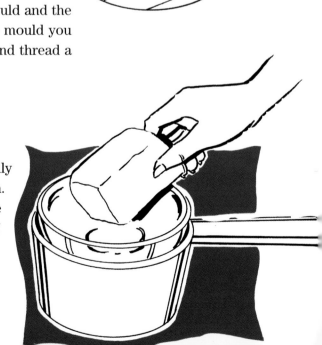

Melt the wax and stearin separately over water. It is generally recommended that you use ten parts wax to one part stearin. Any less and it will be difficult to remove the candle from the mould as stearin is what aids the contraction and release of the wax.

MAKING THE CANDLE

Experts say you should add the wax dye to the stearin and then pour this into the melted wax. I have been in a real rush before and chucked the whole lot into one pan to melt together and the candle has turned out fine but I may have just been lucky. Be wary of wax dye - the set candle will look paler than in melted wax form. Add a bit at a time. When the wax has fully melted pour it evenly into the centre of the mould. Tap the mould gently to release any air bubbles.

SETTING AND TOPPING UP

I just leave my candles in a cool place to set although you can speed the process up by putting them into the refrigerator or in a basin of water up to the level of the wax in the mould. As wax sets it contracts and you may find it sinks in the middle around the wick. Poke holes in the surface of the candle and pour on a little more molten wax to level out the top and leave to set again.

REMOVING THE CANDLE

Never try to take a candle out of the mould until it is completely set and the mould cold to the touch. Remember to remove any mould seal and to cut the wick knot. Remove the rod or skewer and trim the wick to approximately 5mm and then gently shake the mould upside-down and the candle should slide out easily

SHELL CANDLES

YOU WILL NEED

Oyster shells

Pre-waxed wicks

Paraffin wax

Stearin

Cocktail sticks

Saucepans

A friend of mine, Suzy Pass, makes these all the time and ingeniously cuts out all the fuss by melting down shop-bought nightlight candles after she has taken out the wick and wick disc. She simply places them in the empty shell and pours in the wax.

SHELL CANDLES

When we first married we owned a shellfish restaurant in Cornwall, and one popular dish on the menu was oysters from the nearby Duchy Oyster Farm at Helford. I wish I'd known how easy it was to make these candles, especially Suzy's way, otherwise I wouldn't have thrown out the millions of empty oyster and scallop shells.

DECORATED AND SCENTED CANDLES

YOU WILL NEED

Paraffin wax

Stearin

Yellow dye

Wicking

Mould

Rods or skewers (2)

Plastic clay or mould seal

Small lipped jug

Scissors

Dried lavender

Pressed leaves

Slices of orange, cinnamon sticks, cloves etc.

Use the step-by-step instructions to make large basic candles and when they are set decorate them using the tips for decoration in the technique section.

To stick the lavender on, use spray glue on the candle surface and roll the candle on the dried flowers before dipping in the wax to fix. Don't forget to add the essence at the melting wax stage when making the candle. Dry slices of orange in a cool oven for 30 minutes.

DECORATED AND SCENTED CANDLES

Candles are no longer just for the lighting! They have become decorative items of beauty in themselves. You can make them in every colour of the rainbow, scent them with essential oils and mix in with the wax, herbs and spices and other decorations.

FLOATING CANDLES

YOU WILL NEED

Paraffin wax

Stearin

Candle dye(s)

Moulds - I used various bottle tops

Mould sealer

Wicks

Wick discs

Glass beads

A large glass bowl

Saucepans

A jug

Scissors

The joy of these is that you need very little wax - approximately 70g of paraffin wax and 7g of stearin per mould. My favourite mould is a bulbous top from a bottle of bath foam. The same brand shampoo has a smaller top in the same shape.

FLOATING CANDLES

Put these as a centrepiece or on a hallway table to greet guests. The magical mix of lit candles floating in water with the sparkle of glass beads underneath never fails to be effective. Try adding candle scent too.

WHY STOP THERE?

I'm sure you have already got lots of ideas of what sort
of candles you want to make next.

CLAY

Making items from clay is perhaps not the first thing you would think of to tackle in an evening. Visions of potters' wheels, firing kilns and complicated glazes are enough to put anyone off when you are looking for a craft to while away a couple of free hours' spare time. But fear not, some of the wonder new self-hardening or oven-bake modelling materials will allow you to really get stuck into clay and discover how brilliantly versatile this pliable substance is, and how easily you can create great items for your home or as gifts for friends. I have used a selection of the materials on the market but I recommend that you have a good look at what is available in your local craft store because new products are constantly coming onto the market. The three projects I suggest are very simple to make and use a variety of techniques.

31

THE ORIGINS OF CLAY MODELLLING

Because the use of clay is so very ancient we can only speculate as to how it was first discovered. Since, logically, most communities established their small settlements near rivers the raw material would have been virtually underfoot.

The earliest found pottery in Syria has been dated as somewhere between 7,000 and 8,000BC. Of course, even though it has fragmented, it must have been fired to make it hard enough to withstand virtually any amount of time.

It is a fanciful, but pleasing, thought to imagine some basic pot made with woven reeds and coated with clay to give it strength, falling into the open fire on the homestead and emerging later from the dying embers a stronger, harder version of its former self. How long do you think it took those ancient people to work out that this was the way to make useful jars and vessels for cooking and eating out of?

It was only a matter of time before they discovered that as well as making functional containers, they could also create decorative pieces, and it is from the drawings and writings on pottery remains that have been found that we have been able to learn so much about ancient civilisations.

In fact, clay formed the first books with tablets covered in writing found in Egypt dating back from 3,000BC. The clay tiles measured about five inches long and were written on using a stylus while the clay was still wet. Longer texts meant that several tablets had to be used linked together by number or catchwords. These would then either be dried in the sun or baked in a kiln.

It wouldn't have taken long for clay to become very widely used once its properties had been discovered. The first pots, made purely from clay, were probably coil pots - a rolled rope of clay was wound round and round and then the surface smoothed over and decorated.

This technique would have been used to make large pots for storing grain and for funeral urns for ashes. The Eastern leaders, the Emperors and Pharaohs, who wanted to be buried surrounded by them, commissioned large pots. These have provided a font of information about the ancient world when discovered by archaeologists. Clay was also much used in Africa where it was sculpted into terracotta raffia and mud to create religious masks and statues.

It is believed that the methods of glazing pottery were also discovered by accident. Natural pigments are in the earth and perhaps, when being heated by a wood fire, some ash stuck to a pot and it emerged with a shiny coating. Today, there are many different colours and types of glaze you can use. No glazing is tackled in this book because you do need a degree of technical knowhow and a kiln! If you really want to have a go at using real clay it's worth noting that you can often submit your creation for firing in the kiln at a local technical college that runs pottery courses.

It is said that clay is the earth material with the history of the widest use. Now, with the modern self-hardening and oven-bake clays, it is enjoying a real revival as an accessible home craft.

Sponges

Rolling pin

Bowl for water

Wooden work board

Knife

Clay cutter

Strips of wood

Modelling tools

Clay scraper

Round objects to wrap clay around

Paints

Brushes

E Q U I P M E N T

Much of the equipment you will need for modelling with clay can be adapted from items in your kitchen. A word of warning though, don't use them for cooking or eating out of afterwards.

First of all, of course, you need **clay.** There are various types on the market so read the instructions for drying and hardening and choose the one that suits you best. You can buy brightly coloured ones or natural tones, which need painting. You will probably have to buy special **paints**, as normal paints aren't always suitable.

Whatever clay you buy, you will end up needing to wipe down afterwards, but you will need a **sponge** for purposes other than clearing up - **natural sponges** are very useful for smoothing surfaces. The **bowl** is for water to dampen the sponge and I like to work on a **wooden working surface** and have consigned a large meat block for the purpose. Sticking with wood, I find a **wooden rolling** pin works better than a plastic one and that is used, of course, for rolling out flat slabs. The **wooden strips** are just pieces of thin battening that I use as a guide for the clay sheets and there is a variety of clay **modelling tools** you can buy to cut and mark your item. A **clay scraper,** which is a kidney-shaped disc used for smoothing, is useful but, personally, again I find a couple of old **knives** and pieces of cutlery work just as well.

A **clay cutter** is useful and it is easy to make your own from some fishing line of wire and two pieces of wood. It helps also to have a selection of **round objects**, earmarked as suitable sized cylinders to roll your clay around if you are planning to make that sort of pot.

Now I know that the object of the exercise in tackling one of the projects in this book is to end up with something you are really proud of, but I think that much of the real delight in creating things with clay is in the making process. The actual touching and moulding of this pliable material is incredibly therapeutic - to end up with something solid and beautiful that you can then decorate and display is a real added bonus.

TECHNIQUES

Follow the step-by-step guide on page 40 to transform your lump of clay into material ready to make your finished item and then employ one, or several, of these techniques to make your finished item.

CYLINDERS

Roll out your clay between the battens until the width is the measurement you want the height of your cylinder to be. Tape a piece of paper around a bottle or other container that is the diameter you want and then roll the slab around it, cutting the slab so the edges just overlap. Brush the edges with slip (a paste made by mixing clay and water, see page 41) and press them together. Smooth over the join with a scraper and gently slide the bottle out. You can add a slab base and trim the top to make a container.

PINCH POTS

Take a ball of clay and press your thumb into the middle. Squeeze the side of the ball between your thumb and fingers turning it all the time so the sides become thinner. Work from the bottom to the top, pinching the clay into the shape of pot you want.

C O I L   P O T S

First make your coils by rolling ropes of clay gently from the centre out until they are about 12mm in diameter. Make a base for your pot from a slab of clay and then stick a coil to it with some slip, cutting the ends where they meet. Press the coil to the base.

Repeat the process with more coils, making their ends meet in different places each time and gently pressing together. As the clay is hardening scrape the clay and smooth over with a damp sponge.

S L A B   P O T S

These pots are effectively boxes because you can make straight-sided containers using this technique. Cut out four patterns for the sides and base of the box and lay them on rolled-out slabs of clay. Cut around them with a knife, brush slip along the edges to be joined and slide them together until they stick. Check the instructions for the clay you have bought, but often it is a good idea to let the clay harden a little before doing this. Work on one side at a time and when the box is standing, roll out a thin sausage of clay and press it with some slip along the inside of each join to give it strength. Use a scraper to smooth joins on the outside.

D E C O R A T I O N

There are all sorts of different ways you can decorate your clay before it dries really hard. You can write or draw patterns on it by scratching the surface with a pointed tool. This technique is called sgraffito. You can stipple the surface with a stiff brush or you can stamp patterns into the hardening clay with small rigid items. I once saw a pen top used to brilliant effect to make flower patterns on a bowl.

STEP-BY-STEP

These instructions apply generally to preparing and making something from clay, but make sure you read the instructions on the clay you buy because with so many new artificial modelling and moulding materials on the market they may suggest you use different methods.

PREPARING CLAY

Once you have taken your clay out of its wrapper you will need to make sure it has an even texture and that there are no trapped air bubbles. I tend to buy small amounts of packed clay, but if you have bought a large lump you will need to cut off a workable amount of about two handfuls. Always remember to reseal the bag.

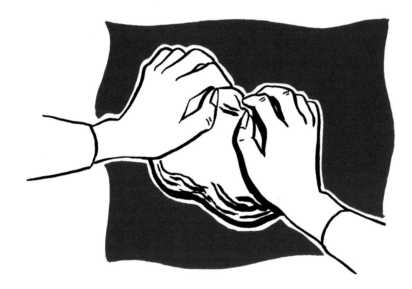

KNEADING CLAY

The technical term for this is 'wedging' the clay. With the heels of your palms press the clay forwards and roll it back several times. Then roll it into a ball and cut through it, checking to see if there are any air pockets. Repeat this until you are happy that the clay is really pliable and bubble-free.

ROLLING CLAY

Flatten your lump of clay by patting it with your hands until it is getting near the thickness you want. Place the wooden battens either side and using your rolling pin roll out from the centre, turning the clay until the slab is the same thickness as the battens.

J O I N I N G   C L A Y

Again check your particular clay instructions to see if they suggest another method, but the usual way is to stick clay pieces together with slip, which is effectively a paste made by mixing clay and water. The easiest way to get this is by making a hollow in a ball of clay with your thumb and then sloshing a wet brush around in the hollow, adding more water, until you have a creamy paste. Make it when you need it and brush the slip on the pieces to be joined, sliding them together several times until you feel them beginning to stick.

C A R V I N G   C L A Y

It is best to let your clay harden slightly before you start to carve on it. Make sure the surface is smooth. Sweeping a flexible metal scraper backwards and forwards should achieve this easily. Then, holding with special modelling tools, or your own customised pointer, like a pen cut and carve either the patterns or lettering of your choice.

M O D E L L I N G

I'm not a big fan of modelling but that may be because I am not naturally artistic. You have to mould your lump of clay into roughly the shape you want and then carve out the features of the object you are making. As it dries you then chisel and carve the finer details. My classic story of getting a model wrong was when an upright stoat, that I thought was quite sweet, was mistaken for a fierce polar bear.

PICTURE FRAME

YOU WILL NEED

One small pack of self-hardening clay in a neutral colour

Battens

Rolling pin

Knife

Pointer or modelling tool

Paint

Brush

A sheet of acetate or mirror if preferred

Photo corners

Glue

A picture hanging hook

Make a cardboard template and use the rolling out method. Embed the picture hook in the clay and slip stick a piece of clay over it to secure it. Stick the acetate and the photo corners on the back of the frame and insert your picture or embed the mirror into clay and secure on the back with tape when dry!

PICTURE FRAME

I made a whole series of these once for a friend with pertinent messages on the frame surrounding relevant pictures. She loved all of them, even the one of her as a teenager dressed in hippy gear with the words 'wild child' inscribed on the frame!

TRINKET BOX

YOU WILL NEED

Clay

Rolling pin

Work board

Knife

Paints

Varnish

Brushes

The pot is made by using the coil method with the base and top cut out from a slab. The flowers are little strips of clay wrapped into tiny swirls with semi-circle petals added around the outside or just diamond shapes with a different colour dot in the middle. The leaves are diamonds too.

TRINKET BOX

This is a really pretty piece of pottery to make and give as a gift. Although it looks quite simple and uses basic methods it will take a bit of patience and nimble fingers to get the flowers right. Spend a bit of time arranging the flowers before securing them to get the best effect.

FRIDGE MAGNETS

YOU WILL NEED

Coloured oven-bake clay

Knife

Rolling pin

Work board

Modelling tools

Small magnets

Glue

Use the templates for the night and day magnets, or use long coils to make fancy name magnets for each member of the family. The little magnets to go on the back are easily obtainable from all good craft shops.

FRIDGE MAGNETS

How did we ever live without fridge magnets? The fridge door serves as a real message board in our household.

The kids can help you make these and once you have stuck the magnets on the backs and put them to work, there will be no excuse for notes and memos to be missed when your nearest and dearest go to raid the fridge.

WHY STOP THERE?

What about jewellery, vases, egg-cups, fake food,
wall plaques candle holders and toy figures for
the children to play with?

PLASTER

Welcome to a much neglected craft material - Plaster of Paris. This wonderful medium magically transforms from powder, to liquid, to solid in a matter of minutes. It is most often used in modelling and moulding work as part of the process to use another medium such as clay or metal, but I hope my three project ideas will inspire you to realise the untapped craft potential of this wonderful substance.

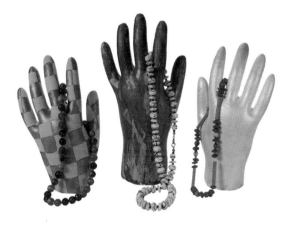

51

THE ORIGINS OF PLASTER OF PARIS

Plaster of Paris (scientific name calcium sulphate dihydrate) is made from gypsum, which is a white mineral rock formed over the course of many millions of years from salt deposits in long-gone inland and underground lakes.

Plaster of Paris is so called because the capital of France is actually built on great areas of gypsum. The gypsum has to be reduced to a fine powder to become plaster. At the powder stage it is heated so that most of the moisture in it is removed. The magic happens when water is added back to the plaster powder and it reverts to the solid it once was.

Plaster is known to have been used over the last 6,000 years all over the world. It has served many and varied a purpose. For example, the Romans used it to preserve bodies and it had another funereal purpose for the Egyptians, who used white plaster on top of mud plaster to decorate the walls of their tombs before sealing them up with their treasures. Another Egyptian connection is the link with the town Alabastron. This, predictably, is where alabaster comes from which is the base substance gypsum in its purest form. Alabaster has been much favoured by sculptors over the centuries and examples of carvings can still be seen in churches and civic buildings in many medieval buildings today.

Paris, being in such an area rich in the raw material, of course has many fine examples of the use of plaster.

It arrived in Britain courtesy of French craftsmen whose work had been admired by the British aristocracy in the Middle Ages. Henry III is said to have been very impressed by the plaster finish on the walls of some buildings in Paris in 1250. He encouraged the craft of the plasterer and there are records of British workmen travelling to France to buy some of the fine materials they needed.

In 1501, The Guild of Plaisterers was granted a charter and by this time plastering was rapidly becoming an art form with distinctive pargeting adorning the walls of even humble dwellings. These began to mark out localities and even today, particularly in counties such as Suffolk, you can see how the skill of the plasterer has contributed to the unique look of the towns and villages with the emblems of acorns, flowers and fleur de lys. It is still a craft that is very much alive today. Recently I was in Suffolk and was amused to see how one householder had commissioned a pargeter to plaster emblems on the front of her home. She had chosen ones that would reflect her family's characteristics. Under her teenage son's bedroom window a plaster Doc Marten boot stood proud from the cob wall.

Historically, plaster has had a secondary role in craft where it has been used as a preliminary material in the process to make a mould before an end item is cast in metal such as bronze.

And, of course, we shouldn't forget its role within the building industry where it is indispensable in wall boarding and fillers.

Plaster

A plastic bucket or bowl

Water

Moulds

Kitchen cloth

Plaster-impregnated cloth

Cardboard

Rubber bands

Knife

Modelling tools

Fine sandpaper

Gesso or primer

Paint and brushes

Glue

EQUIPMENT

Of course the first thing you need is plaster but make sure it is the fine **Plaster of Paris** that is suitable for craft and not the coarser grade used in building work. It is really important to keep your plaster dry because any contact with moisture and it will start solidifying. I like to mix my plaster in a **plastic bucket** because it does harden very quickly and in the early days I ruined a couple of china containers. *Never* work with plaster in your sink because it will block the drains. Never mix fresh plaster in a container which contains some old plaster - the great thing about a flexible plastic bucket is that it is easy to totally remove all the plaster. Plain tap **water** does the job, the colder the better because any heat will speed up the setting process. You'll need to have your **moulds** ready, either shop bought or homespun. For example, the ring hand stand uses a rubber glove. The most important thing to remember is that it has to be rubbery and flexible enough to remove. You can saturate **kitchen cloths** in plaster or buy **ready impregnated fabric strips.**

Cardboard and **rubber bands** are indispensable if you want to prop up your mould, as with the ring hand, and when your plaster is dry you may want to sand it down, carve or decorate it before sticking it onto another item. So you will need **sandpaper**, a **knife** or some **modelling tools**, **primer** or **gesso**, **paints** and **brushes** and possibly **glue.**

Just look at these wonderful pieces of plasterwork. They are the creation of Daniel Birch. Don't think for a minute that you will be able to make anything like this because it takes tremendous skill and precision to make plaster work for you this effectively. However, I guarantee that you will have great fun making the simple projects I have chosen. The actual process of working with plaster is in itself a great experience and never fails to entrance me.

TECHNIQUES

MAKING YOUR OWN MOULD

If you don't want to buy a mould or use one of the ideas suggested in the projects you can make your own mould from clay. Press into a soft slab of clay the object you want to make a plaster cast of e.g. a lemon segment. Add a small wall around the impression to contain the liquid plaster. When the plaster has set and before the clay hardens peel off the mould. Any pieces of clay sticking to the plaster should be either washed off or removed by gently pressing a small ball of soft clay against them until they pull off easily.

TEXTURE

You can actually alter the texture of plaster as you are making it by adding different things, such as rice, sand, sawdust, glitter, herb seeds etc. Never add more than one-third of the amount of plaster and it has to be said that the end product will be weaker as a result. An intriguing bubble effect can be obtained by adding baking powder to your plaster mix. It's fun both to do and look at but I haven't ever found a use for it!

MATERIAL

You can buy special plaster-impregnated strips of fabric that can be shaped and moulded with some fluidity before they set. You can make something similar yourself by dipping loose weave material such as kitchen cloth into liquid plaster and draping it into whatever shape you desire before it dries. Most materials will take plaster well.

A clever idea is to dip big tassels into plaster and when they set paint and gild them into unusual curtain tie-backs. Rope works similarly well and could be used to make an interesting frame around a porthole window.

PAINT

You can actually change the colour of the plaster by adding colourants as you mix the powder into the water. I have found the best method is to use powder paints that you can buy in quantity and quite cheaply. I have also used artists' inks and dyes. An interesting effect is to dribble a strong liquid colour into the plaster just as it begins to turn thick and not to mix it in too much so that you get a marble ripple effect.

CARVING

Plaster is very soft and can be easily sculpted if you find the right tool. You don't chip away, but scrape and scoop. You will need to experiment with different implements and some of the modelling tools meant for use with clay work. However, my favourite carving tool happens to be a very blunt and worn small kitchen knife which proves that you don't always need to spend money to get the right equipment.

SURFACE TEXTURE

Try applying some more plaster when your basic item has completely set. Dab fresh plaster on with a sponge or a stubby paint brush. Try scoring the surface with a wire brush or file. Sand indentations or paint the surface with glue and roll the object in flock, sand or glitter.

STEP-BY-STEP

Let me give you a few tips before you start on the adventure of mixing your first bucket of plaster. You have got about fifteen minutes from the time you sprinkle the plaster powder onto the water until it sets, so read the following step-by-step instructions and then read them again, making sure you have everything you need to hand. On no account try to re-soften hard plaster by adding more water. It won't work.

SPRINKLING THE PLASTER

Now trust me - I have asked everyone there is to ask about the proportions of plaster powder to water and no-one will give me firm and fast rules. They all say it's approximately one to two parts plaster to one part water, which frankly isn't a lot of use if you like to be exact. My experience says it's about one and a half parts plaster to one part water, but then sometimes that mix seems to set too quickly. What I can promise is that very quickly you'll get a 'feel' for mixing plaster. Pour your clean cold water into the plastic bucket or bowl and then sprinkle handfuls of plaster onto the surface of the water as quickly as you can without splashing. Carry on until the plaster is only just breaking the water surface without being absorbed. Never add water to plaster and make sure your plaster is bone dry and free from lumps.

MIXING THE PLASTER

Leave the plaster for a couple of minutes to allow it to completely absorb and then, again quickly, stir the mixture around using either a spoon or, as I prefer, your hand.

The plaster should now be quite creamy and is ready to use. If you are not using the plaster for a mould and plan to instead pour it over an existing model in dribbles you will need to leave the plaster mix to become thicker. Over-mixing at this point could cause air bubbles.

POURING THE PLASTER

Gently pour the liquid plaster into the mould to the required depth. While it is still liquid move the mould gently to get rid of any lurking air pockets which will rise to the surface as air bubbles. Now put to one side to set completely.

SETTING

As the plaster begins to set embed any hooks for hanging or non-plaster additions. You will notice shortly as the plaster hardens that it begins to give off heat. This is a natural chemical reaction. It is possible to speed up the setting time by either making your plaster mix three parts plaster to one part water, by using hot water instead of cold or by using salted water. You can try to slow down the setting time by adding five per cent vinegar to the water. That's the chemistry theory although I have to confess I have never tried it because much of the fun of this craft for me is the race against time. You must leave the plaster for as long as you can before removing from the mould - certainly not before it has stopped giving off heat. I usually leave my plaster creations for at least an hour.

DECORATING

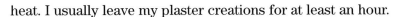

I always paint on a coat of gesso or plain white emulsion to act as a sealant and a primer for my other paints. Then just treat as you would any other straightforward material ready for painting.

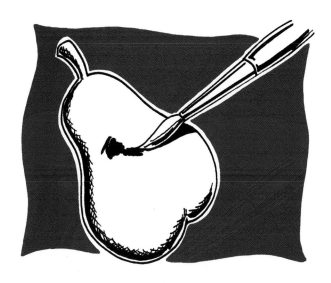

RING STAND

YOU WILL NEED

Plaster

Water

Plastic bucket or bowl

Smallest size rubber glove

Cardboard

Rubber bands

Gesso or primer

Paints and paint brush

Roll the cardboard into a cylinder wide enough for the rubber glove to drop into it and secure with the rubber bands. Place the glove into the cylinder and turn the cuff up over the top. Secure this with another rubber band. Holding the glove and cylinder steady with one hand, carefully pour the mixed liquid plaster into the glove. Leave to set then cut the glove away from the plaster, being careful round the fingers. Level the base so that it stands upright and then decorate.

RING STAND

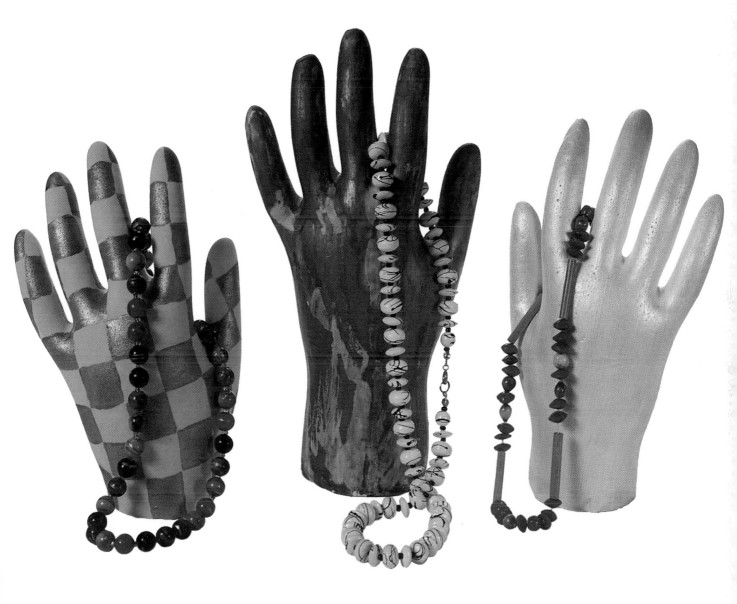

I was as thrilled re-making these hands as an adult as I was when Mrs Bath, my art teacher at school, first taught us how to use plaster. Mind you, as they waited to be decorated around the kitchen they got some very strange looks from visitors.

BOWL

YOU WILL NEED

Six kitchen cloths

Plaster

Water

Plastic bucket or bowl

A plastic bowl to drape over

Gesso or primer

Paints and brushes

This is where you can experiment with the dip and drape technique using fabric. Work as quickly as you can and drape the cloths soaked in liquid plaster either over the upturned bowl or around the inside and swagged along the top as a rim.

THE BOWL

I discovered that kitchen cloth was a good alternative to the shop-bought impregnated fabric when I ran out of the commercial variety before I had finished a small pot-pourri container. No-one could spot the difference. Be warned though - making this bowl is a messy business. However, it is great fun and I hope you agree that the end result is strikingly individual!

FRUIT PICTURE FRAME

YOU WILL NEED

Basic frame

Fruit moulds

Plaster

Water

Brushes

Paint

Bostic adhesive

Varnish

This is a very simple but effective way to decorate a basic shop-bought frame. Use moulds found in any craft shop, fill with plaster, and when set carefully pop out. Paint, then arrange round the frame and when happy stick into place.

FRUIT PICTURE FRAME

This is a clever way to enhance a poor picture frame and really create an individual accessory for your kitchen. Instead of a picture, what about a mirror?

WHY STOP THERE?

I hope you have enjoyed your encounter with plaster and agree that it is a marvellous medium to work with. Never mind creating something in an evening - you've just got plaster in a mere fifteen minutes! Of course, plaster craftsmen spend many hours making the often intricate moulds and you would need to have proper tuition to learn how to do that, but I hope you have been inspired to make some more simple projects.

KITS

I have developed a range of kits complementary to this book. Each kit contains everything that you will need to make something with wax, clay and plaster, and at the end of your endeavours I'm sure you will have something beautiful.

Candlemaking: Lighten up your life with all you need in this kit to make home-made candles. The moulds, the wax and comprehensive instructions will get you on your way to making candles suitable for all occasions.

Contents:	Paraffin wax
	Stearin
	Candle dye
	Upright candle mould
	Moulds for floating candles
	Scented candle essence
	Wicks
	Wick discs
	Rods
	Dried lavender
	Pressed leaves

Clay: This kit gives you the opportunity to try your hand literally at clay modelling. The special air-hardening medium included will allow you to try the projects in the book, attempt your own creations or just experience the therapeutic qualities of working with this wonderful substance.

Contents	Self-hardening clay
	A modelling tool
	A rolling pin
	Yellow, blue and red paint
	Silver paint
	Brush
	Sponge
	Fridge magnet

Plaster: You don't need to break a limb to appreciate working with plaster. There is everything you need to experiment with this magical medium and create lovely things for yourself, your home or friends and family.

Contents:	Plaster of Paris
	Rubber glove
	A pot of Gesso
	Plaster cloth
	Paints
	Brush

All the above are available from all good craft stores and by mail order from:

Really Vital Productions Ltd
PO Box 330
Slough SL2 3FH
Telephone orders call the orderline on 01753 648780

INDEX

A
Alabaster 52

Alabastron 52
Aromatic oils 14, 15

B
Balanphora 12
Beeswax 19
Birch, Daniel 57
Brazilian palm 12

C
Candle dye 14, 15
Candle power 13
Carnauba 12
Clay cutter 34
Clay scraper 34
Clay tiles 32
Coil pots 38
Cylinder pots 38

E
Egyptian candlesticks 12
Equipment for
- clay 34, 35
- plaster 54, 55
- wax 14, 15

G
Guild of Plaisterers 53
Gypsum 52

H
Henry III 53
Herbs 15
History
- clay 32, 33
- plaster 52, 53
 wax 12, 13

M
Modelling tools 35
Mould seal 14
Moulds 14
Multicoloured candles 18

O
Ozokerite 12

P
Paraffin wax 14, 15
Pargeter 53
Phoenicians 13
Pigments 33
Pinch pots 38
Projects
- floating candles 26
- fridge magnets 46
- fruit picture frame 66
- picture frame 42
- plaster bowl 64
- ring hand 62
- scented candles 24
- shell candles 22
- trinket box 44

R
Rods 14, 15

S
Sgraffito 39
Slab pots 39
Stage lighting 13
Stearic acid 13
Stearin 14
Step-by-Step
- clay 40, 41
- plaster 58, 59
- wax 20, 21
Suppliers 73

T
Techniques
- clay 38, 39
- plaster 58, 59
- wax 18, 19

W
Whipped wax 18
Wick discs 14, 15
Wicks 14, 15 20

EQUIPMENT AND SUPPLIERS

We are now very well served in this country for craft suppliers and retailers. There are quite a few large stores that sell practically everything you need to make your projects, and just wandering around looking at all their stock will give you loads of other ideas and inspire you to be more ambitious. I'll also bet that somewhere in your locality there will be a small craft or artists' suppliers who will probably have what you need or, if not, will certainly order it for you and take a real interest in what you are making.

I have found that the people who work in both sorts of outlets are most helpful and encouraging. If all else fails, there are loads of people selling craft components by mail order and their addresses can usually be found in the back of any of the craft magazines. The following are a few names and addresses of people and products I have used.

SUPPLIERS

Manufacturers, Importers and Wholesalers

Atlascraft
4 Plumtree St
The Lace Market
Nottingham
NG1 1JL
For your local suppliers please call customer services :
Tel: 0115 9415280
Fax: 0115 9415281

A wide range of products covering most crafts. Main importers of Deka paints. Their range is available at John Lewis Partnership Shops.

ColArt Fine Art & Graphics Ltd
Whitefriars Avenue
Harrow
Middlesex
HA3 5RH

For your local suppliers please call customer services:
Tel: 0181 427 4343
Fax: 0181 863 7177

A large portfolio of well-known branded fine art materials including Winsor & Newton, Lefranc & Bourgeois and Dryad.

Daler Rowney Ltd
P.O.Box 10
Bracknell
Berkshire
RG12 8ST

For your local suppliers please call customer services :
Tel: 01344 424621
Fax: 01344 486511

Largest manufacturer of a fully comprehensive range of colours, brushes, surfaces and artists and craft accessories

Philip & Tacey Ltd
North Way
Andover
Hampshire
SP10 5BA

For your local suppliers please call customer services :
Tel: 01264 332171
Fax: 01264 332226
E-Mail: sales@philipandtacey.co.uk

One of the longest established family firms in the arts and craft business. They carry a large range of stock and are the importers of the well-known Pebeo range of paints.

SUPPLIERS

Manufacturers, Importers and Wholesalers (continued)

Inscribe Ltd
Unit 52
The Woolmer Industrial Estate
Bordon
Hampshire
GU35 9QE

For your local suppliers please call customer services:
Tel: 01420 475747
Fax: 01420 489867

Sole importers of Fimo modelling clays and supplier of most art, craft and hobby materials.

Retail, Mail Order and Training Workshops

Cats Group
PO Box 12
Saxmundham
Suffolk
Tel: 01728 648717

Mail order specialist. A comprehensive range of all materials needed for the projects in this book.

Creative World
The Bishop Centre
Bath Rd
Taplow
Berkshire
SL6 0NY
Tel: 01628 661331
and at

Creative World
The Galleries
Bristol
Tel: 0117 929 7775

These are one of the new expanding chains of larger shops. They carry thousands of lines covering all crafts. Good for browsing!

Plasterworks
160 East Reach
Taunton
Somerset
TA1 3HT
Tel: 01823 326694

A shop selling fine hand-made plasterware and gifts. Most are made on the premises including a range of architectural mouldings for house renovation.

Hobbicraft
Ferndown
Bournemouth
Tel: 01202 596100

A rapidly expanding chain of out-of-town superstores.

Nexus presents "Create It .....In an Evening", a series of books developed by Caroline Righton (your regular columnist on *Popular Crafts* TV presenter, producer, journalist and craft specialist), in response to the growing demand for innovative craft books suitable for today's busy lifestyle.

Other titles in this series

If you have enjoyed making the projects in this book, why not try your hand at other crafts? Other titles in this series include:

Create it with Paper in an Evening — Nine projects for making things with paper - découpage, papier mâché and hand-made paper. All are easily achievable by beginners with simple illustrated instructions and full colour throughout.

ISBN 1-85486-175-1

Create it with Paint in an Evening — Another nine easy projects for painting on silk, glass or fabric. Again split into three sections each one comprising an introduction, equipment list, techniques and a step-by-step guide to the basic skills needed.

ISBN 1-85486-174-3

Create it with Thread in an Evening — In this book Caroline offers the option of applying your skills to three different mediums: quilting, appliqué and cross-stitch. All the projects are easily achievable by beginnners and great fun for all skill levels.

ISBN 1-85486-176-X

All the above titles should be obtainable from good bookshops. In the event of difficulty please contact the Books Division, Nexus Special Interests Ltd., Nexus House, Azalea Drive, Swanley, Kent BR8 8HU Tel: 01322 660070

NEW TITLE FROM NEXUS SPECIAL INTERESTS

Alice and Daisy: Edwardian rag doll sisters to make and dress
Valerie Janitch

The basic Alice & Daisy dolls are simple enough for a beginner to make and equally easy to dress, with charming colour photographs that follow Alice & Daisy through their busy social diary. Whether it's lessons, shopping, tea in the country, a birthday party or just retiring to bed, an appropriate outfit is a necessity (plus beribboned underpinnings, of course!). Be warned! Once you have made the fashion conscious rag dolls, they won't allow you to resist the temptation to make their entire wardrobe. This book gives you the instructions to make the pretty and romantic Edwardian fashions that are such an important part of their sophisticated lifestyle. Alice & Daisy may be rag dolls, but *mere* rag dolls they are not!

To be published Autumn 1998.